AI Made Simple

Practical Tools to Enhance Your Everyday Life

Diana Kara Lynn Sage

ISBN: 9798316379224

Disclaimer:
This book was created with AI assistance and refined by the author. While every effort has been made to provide accurate and up-to-date information, the author and publisher assume no responsibility for errors, omissions, or outcomes resulting from the use of the content. Readers should conduct their own research and consult professionals where appropriate before relying on any AI tools, services, or strategies mentioned.

First Edition

Published by Diana Kara Lynn Sage

Table of Contents

- AI Lifestyle & Wellness Tools
- AI Fitness Tools
- AI Personal Coaching & Virtual Trainer Tools
- AI Tools for Injury Prevention & Recovery
- AI Nutrition Tools
- AI Supplement & Wellness Tools
- AI Mental Health & Stress Management Tools
- AI Sleep Optimization Tools
- AI Medical Tools
- AI Medication & Chronic Disease Management Tools

- AI Task & Project Management Tools
- AI Scheduling & Time Management Tools
- AI Email & Communication Tools
- AI Focus & Productivity Tools
- AI Writing & Documentation Tools
- AI Learning & Knowledge Tools
- AI Personal Productivity Tools
- AI Work-Life Balance & Well-Being Tools

- AI Networking Tools
- AI Long-Distance Relationship Tools
- AI Emotional & Conflict Resolution Tools

Chapter 6: AI for Education & Learning

- AI Study & Time Management Tools
- AI Learning Platforms
- AI Reading Tools
- AI Gamified Learning Tools
- AI Homework & Tutoring Tools
- AI Test Prep Tools
- AI Summarization Tools
- AI Skill & Career Training Platforms
- AI Language Learning Apps
- AI Writing & Research Tools
- AI Accessibility Tools
- AI Grading & Assessment Tools

Chapter 7: AI for Creativity & Content Creation

- AI Writing Tools
- AI Art & Design Tools
- AI Music & Audio Tools
- AI Video Editing Tools

- AI Social Media Tools
- AI Storytelling Tools
- AI Collaboration & Workflow Tools
- AI Branding & Marketing Tools
- AI Copyright & Protection Tools

Chapter 8: AI for Entrepreneurship & Business Growth

- AI Resume & Cover Letter Tools
- AI Interview Prep Tools
- AI Job Search & Application Tracking Tools
- AI Learning & Skill Development Platforms
- AI Tools for Freelancers
- AI Automation Tools
- AI Workplace Productivity Tools
- AI Hiring & Team Management Tools
- AI Chatbot & Customer Support Tools
- AI Marketing & Advertising Tools
- AI Marketing Tools
- AI Lead Generation Tools
- AI Finance & Accounting Tools
- AI Salary & Career Growth Tools
- AI E-commerce & Product Development Tools
- AI Business Intelligence Tools
- AI Branding & Social Media Tools
- AI Legal Tools

Introduction:

Welcome to the AI Revolution

Artificial Intelligence is no longer just a futuristic concept from sci-fi movies—it's here and you can use it to transform the way you live, work, and create. From voice assistants like Alexa to powerful AI-driven art tools, this technology is making everyday life easier, more productive, and even more creative. A lot of people don't realize how much this expanding technology can reduce stress in their everyday life.

This book is your guide to unlocking the full potential of many AI tools. Whether you're looking to save time, make money, boost creativity, or simply make daily tasks easier, AI has something to offer you.

In this book, we'll explore how you can use Artificial Intelligence to:

- **Enhance productivity** by automating tasks, scheduling, and even writing for you.

- **Improve personal life** through smart budgeting, health tracking, and home automation.
- **Unlock creativity** with AI-powered art, music, and content creation tools.
- **Help build businesses and side hustles** by automating marketing, content creation, and product development.

By the end of this book, you'll not only understand AI a lot more, but you'll know exactly how to use it to **enhance your life and even create new income streams.** Let's dive in and look at all the ways to make your life easier!

Chapter 1

AI for Health & Wellness

AI is transforming the way we track health, improve fitness, manage mental well-being, and access medical care.Whether you're looking to lose weight, build muscle, improve mental health, or create a sustainable fitness routine, AI-powered tools can help you optimize your approach with personalized recommendations and real-time insights.

AI Lifestyle & Wellness Tools:

AI assists in habit tracking, lifestyle coaching, and overall well-being improvement.

- **Youper AI** – AI-powered emotional well-being tracking.
- **Happify AI** – AI-enhanced positive psychology exercises.

- **Evolve AI** – AI-driven habit coaching and personal growth insights.
- **Fabulous AI** – AI-powered behavior change and habit-building.
- **Eight Sleep AI** – AI-driven sleep optimization for recovery and longevity.
- **InsideTracker AI** – AI-driven blood biomarker analysis for longevity.
- **Viome AI** – AI-powered gut microbiome analysis and dietary optimization.

✔ **Example:** AI can create customized self-care plans to improve mental and physical well-being.

AI for Fitness & Workout Optimization

AI-powered fitness tools analyze body metrics, suggest personalized workout routines, and track progress to help individuals stay fit.

AI Fitness Tools:

- **Fitbod AI** – Generates custom workout plans based on strength and progress.
- **Tempo AI** – AI-driven personal training with real-time feedback.
- **Oura Ring** – AI-based fitness and recovery tracking.
- **Zing Coach AI** – AI-powered virtual personal trainer.

- **Apple Watch AI** – AI-driven heart rate monitoring and fitness tracking.
- **Fitbit AI** – AI-powered activity tracking and health insights.
- **Garmin AI** – AI-enhanced sports and performance analytics.
- **Freeletics AI** – Generates personalized bodyweight workout plans.
- **Jefit AI** – AI-powered workout tracking and optimization.
- **Aaptiv AI** – AI-enhanced audio-guided workouts.
- **Whoop AI** – AI-driven fitness tracking and recovery insights.
- **Nike Training Club AI** – AI-driven coaching and workout tracking.

AI Personal Coaching & Virtual Trainer Tools:

- **Peloton AI** – AI-driven cycling and fitness coaching.
- **Trainerize AI** – AI-enhanced virtual personal training.
- **Kemtai AI** – AI-powered computer vision for workout corrections.
- **Tempo AI** – AI-driven home gym with real-time coaching.
- **Aaptiv AI** – AI-enhanced audio coaching for workouts.
- **Fiture AI** – AI-powered interactive fitness mirror.

✔ **Example:** AI can adjust your workout plan in real time based on your fitness level and recovery needs, improving your workouts to get better results.

AI Tools for Injury Prevention & Recovery:

- **Hinge Health AI** – AI-powered physical therapy and pain management.
- **Kaia Health AI** – AI-driven back pain and posture correction program.
- **SWORD Health AI** – AI-enhanced virtual physical therapy.
- **Recover AI** – AI-powered injury diagnosis and recovery tracking.
- **Whoop AI** – AI-enhanced fitness and recovery optimization.
- **MoveU AI** – AI-driven body alignment coaching.
- **Perfect Posture AI** – AI-driven posture tracking and correction.
- **VAY Fitness AI** – AI-powered movement analysis to prevent injuries.

✔ **Example:** AI can detect poor posture while sitting or exercising and provide real-time correction tips.

AI for Nutrition & Meal Planning

AI can help create personalized diet plans, track calorie intake, and suggest healthy recipes.

AI Nutrition Tools:

- **MyFitnessPal AI & Lifesum** – AI-powered calorie tracking and meal planning.
- **Suggestic AI** – AI-generated meal plans based on dietary preferences.
- **Foodvisor AI** – AI-powered food recognition for nutrition tracking.
- **Whisk AI** – AI that generates smart grocery lists and recipes.
- **Lifesum AI** – AI-generated personalized diet plans.
- **Eat This Much AI** – AI-driven automatic meal planning.
- **Lumen AI** – AI-driven metabolism tracking for weight management.
- **Foodvisor AI** – AI-powered food recognition and portion tracking.
- **Yazio AI** – AI-driven calorie tracking and nutrition analysis.

✔ **Example:** AI can create meal plans tailored to weight loss, muscle gain, or specific health goals.

AI Supplement & Wellness Tools:

- **Care. AI** – AI-powered personalized vitamin and supplement plans.
- **Baze AI** – AI-enhanced nutrient deficiency tracking.
- **Persona AI** – AI-driven daily supplement customization.
- **Rootine AI** – AI-powered DNA-based nutrition recommendations.

✔ **Example:** AI can analyze your diet, genetics, and lifestyle to create a custom supplement plan.

AI for Mental Health & Stress Management

AI-driven mental health tools provide guidance, therapy support, and stress-relief exercises.

AI Mental Health Tools:

- **Wysa AI** – AI-powered emotional support chatbot for mental well-being.
- **Woebot AI** – AI-driven CBT (Cognitive Behavioral Therapy) chatbot.
- **Calm AI & Headspace AI** – AI-powered meditation and mindfulness tools.
- **Replika AI** – AI companion for social and emotional support.
- **Youper AI** – AI-powered cognitive behavioral therapy (CBT) assistant.
- **Headspace AI** – AI-enhanced guided meditation and mindfulness coaching.

✔ **How AI Helps:**

■ Provides **daily mental health check-ins and coping strategies.**

■ Guides users through **breathing exercises and mindfulness routines.**

■ Uses AI chatbots to **offer emotional support in real time.**

AI for Sleep Tracking & Recovery

AI helps analyze sleep patterns, improve rest quality, and offer personalized sleep advice.

AI Sleep Optimization Tools:

- **Sleep Cycle AI** – AI-powered smart alarm that tracks sleep patterns.
- **Oura Ring AI & Eight Sleep** – AI-driven sleep tracking and temperature control.
- **Rise Science AI** – AI that optimizes sleep cycles for better productivity.
- **Pillow AI** – AI-powered sleep tracking and analysis.
- **Dodow AI** – AI-driven breathing exercises for faster sleep.
- **SleepScore AI** – AI-powered sleep analysis and improvement suggestions.
- **Whoop AI** – AI-enhanced sleep performance tracking.
- **ShutEye AI** – AI-driven sleep sound analysis and improvement.

✔ **Example:** AI can detect sleep disruptions and provide insights to enhance sleep quality for better overall health.

AI for Medical Diagnostics & Healthcare

AI is being used in healthcare to detect diseases, identify health risks, track symptoms, assist in diagnosis, and provide telehealth services.

AI Medical Tools:

- **Ada AI** – AI symptom checker for preliminary diagnosis.
- **Buoy Health AI** – AI-driven healthcare advice and symptom tracking.
- **IBM Watson Health** – AI-powered medical data analysis for doctors.
- **SkinVision AI** – AI that analyzes skin conditions for early disease detection.
- **Huma AI** – AI-enhanced remote patient monitoring.
- **Qardio AI** – AI-powered heart health tracking.
- **QBio AI** – AI-enhanced full-body health scanning and risk analysis.
- **K Health AI** – AI-driven medical insights and virtual doctor consultations.
- **Teladoc AI** – AI-enhanced virtual doctor visits.
- **Mayo Clinic AI** – AI-driven disease prediction and diagnosis support.
- **Babylon AI** – AI-powered healthcare assistant for remote consultations.
- **Fitbit AI** – AI-powered heart rate and activity tracking.
- **Apple Health AI** – AI-driven health insights and alerts.
- **ZOE AI** – AI-enhanced gut health and metabolic tracking.

✔ **Example:** AI can help detect potential health conditions early, allowing users to seek professional help faster.

AI Medication & Chronic Disease Management Tools:

AI tools help patients track medications, monitor chronic conditions, and predict health risks.

- **Medisafe AI** – AI-powered medication reminders and tracking.
- **Diabits AI** – AI-driven diabetes management and glucose monitoring.
- **MyTherapy AI** – AI-enhanced chronic disease tracking and adherence support.
- **Propeller AI** – AI-powered asthma and COPD symptom tracking.

✔ **Example:** AI can remind patients to take medications and analyze health trends to detect early warning signs.

AI as Your Ultimate Health & Fitness Partner

AI is revolutionizing fitness, nutrition, mental health, sleep, and medical diagnostics, making health management more accessible and personalized. Whether you want to optimize workouts, improve mental well-being, or track health metrics, AI provides real-time insights and automation to enhance your well-being.

Chapter 2

AI for Productivity & Time Management

Though time is our most precious asset, daily demands leave us feeling perpetually shortchanged, spending a currency whose total we can never truly know.

AI is a powerful tool for increasing efficiency, organization, and time management. Whether you're an entrepreneur, freelancer, or busy parent, AI can help you automate tasks, prioritize work, and optimize your schedule.

AI for Task & Project Management

AI-powered tools help users stay organized, manage projects, and boost productivity by streamlining daily tasks. Instead of spending hours on repetitive work like responding to emails, setting reminders, or organizing files, AI can automate these processes—freeing up time for more important tasks. For example,

AI can analyze email content to suggest quick, relevant responses and even categorize emails based on sender, keywords, and importance to keep your inbox organized. If you're short on time, AI can also summarize lengthy emails into brief, actionable points. Here are some great tools to help you save time and stay productive.

AI Task & Project Management Tools:

- **Notion AI** – AI-enhanced task organization and note-taking.
- **Trello AI** – AI-driven workflow automation for task management.
- **Asana AI** – AI-powered project planning and collaboration.
- **ClickUp AI** – AI-enhanced productivity and goal tracking.
- **Zapier:** Connects apps like Gmail, Slack, and Trello to automate workflows.
- **IFTTT:** Automates daily tasks (e.g., "Turn off phone notifications during meetings").

✔ **Example:** AI can suggest deadlines, automate task assignments, and provide productivity insights.

AI for Scheduling & Time Management

Gone are the days of manually planning your week. Sure some of us still use the good old fashioned magnetic calendar for the fridge, and no doubt the majority put almost every important event in their phone's calendar to have on hand at all times. AI-driven calendars can almost seem like you have your own personal assistant as it can suggest optimal meeting times, automate scheduling, and even predict your most productive hours.

AI Scheduling & Time Management Tools:

- **Reclaim AI** – AI-powered smart scheduling and time blocking.
- **Clockwise AI** – AI-driven calendar management for optimal productivity.
- **x.ai AI** – AI-powered meeting scheduling and reminders.
- **Motion AI** – AI-driven task prioritization and automatic scheduling.
- **Google Calendar AI:** Recommends meeting slots and auto-schedules based on past behavior.

How to Use It:

1. Sync your email and work calendar.
2. Let AI auto-schedule your day based on your tasks.
3. Set AI reminders to avoid missing deadlines.

✔ **Example:** AI can automatically schedule meetings, find the best time slots, and optimize your daily workflow.

AI for Email & Communication Management

AI tools streamline email handling by automating responses, summarizing emails, and prioritizing messages.

AI Email & Communication Tools:

- **Gmail AI & Smart Compose** – AI-assisted email drafting and suggestions.
- **Superhuman AI** – AI-powered email management and prioritization.
- **Grammarly AI** – AI-enhanced grammar and email writing improvement.
- **SaneBox AI** – AI-driven email filtering and organization.

✔ **Example:** AI can summarize emails, draft responses, and highlight urgent messages.

AI for Focus & Distraction Management

AI helps users stay focused by blocking distractions and promoting deep work.

✔ **How AI Helps:**
■ Automates scheduling to **avoid time conflicts.**
■ Suggests the **best times** for focused work.
■ Provides **AI-generated task lists** based on urgency & importance.

AI Focus & Productivity Tools:

- **RescueTime AI** – AI-driven time tracking and focus analysis.
- **Forest AI** – AI-powered focus app that encourages distraction-free work.
- **Freedom AI** – AI-enhanced website and app blocker for productivity.
- **Brain.fm AI** – AI-generated focus music for deep concentration.
- **Serene:** Creates a deep work session by combining focus tools with ambient noise and task management.
- **Pomodoro timers:** Helps work in focused bursts and avoid burnout.
- **Reclaim.ai** – AI auto-schedules your calendar based on priorities.
- **Notion AI** – AI-enhanced notes, to-do lists, and project management.
- **Microsoft 365 Copilot & Google Gemini AI** – AI-powered email and document management.

✔ **Example:** AI can analyze work habits and suggest strategies to improve focus.

AI for Writing & Documentation

AI-powered tools assist with writing reports, generating documents, and automating note-taking.

AI Writing & Documentation Tools:

- **ChatGPT AI** – AI-powered content creation and note-taking.
- **Otter.ai** – AI-generated meeting transcriptions and summaries.
- **Scribe AI** – AI-powered process documentation and SOP creation.
- **Evernote AI** – AI-enhanced note organization and search.
- **Obsidian AI** – AI-powered knowledge management tool.
- **AudioPen** – AI converts voice notes into structured text.

✔ **Example:** AI can automatically transcribe meetings, summarize notes, and generate reports.

AI for Learning & Knowledge Management

AI-driven platforms enhance learning, research, and information retention.

AI Learning & Knowledge Tools:

- **Perplexity AI** – AI-powered research assistant and Q&A.
- **Elicit AI** – AI-driven academic and business research assistant.
- **Anki AI** – AI-powered flashcards for memory retention.
- **Mem AI** – AI-enhanced personal knowledge management.

✔ **Example:** AI can help students and professionals research and summarize complex topics.

AI for Personal Productivity & Life Optimization

AI can analyze habits, optimize routines, and improve personal productivity.

AI Personal Productivity Tools:

- **Google Assistant & Siri AI** – AI-powered virtual assistants for daily tasks.
- **Toggl AI** – AI-enhanced time tracking for productivity insights.
- **Fathom AI** – AI-generated personal coaching and habit tracking.
- **Endel AI** – AI-driven soundscapes for relaxation and focus.

✔ **Example:** AI can help create a personalized daily routine based on productivity patterns.

AI for Work-Life Balance & Well-Being

AI assists in reducing burnout, managing stress, and improving overall well-being.

AI Work-Life Balance & Well-Being Tools:

- **Calm AI** – AI-powered meditation and stress management.
- **Headspace AI** – AI-driven mindfulness and relaxation coaching.
- **Wysa AI** – AI-powered mental health chatbot for emotional support.

- **Habitica AI** – AI-enhanced habit tracking and gamification.

✔ **Example:** AI can suggest mindfulness exercises, track habits, and promote healthy work-life balance.

AI as Your Personal Productivity Assistant

With AI, managing time no longer has to be a struggle. By integrating AI-driven calendars, automation tools, and focus apps, you can **work smarter, not harder**—getting more done in less time without having to remember every task. Making it even more possible for you to keep climbing that hill and living your dream.

Chapter 3

AI for Home Automation & Smart Living

AI-powered home automation is transforming the way we live, manage our homes, and enhance daily convenience. From smart assistants to energy-efficient systems, AI helps optimize security, comfort, and efficiency.

AI-Powered Smart Assistants

AI assistants like Alexa, Google Assistant, and Siri integrate with smart home devices to automate tasks and provide hands-free control.

AI Smart Assistants:

- **Amazon Alexa AI** – Controls smart devices, schedules tasks, and provides information.
- **Google Assistant AI** – Voice-activated home automation and AI-powered responses.
- **Apple Siri AI** – Integrates with Apple smart home devices.

- **Samsung Bixby AI** – AI for Samsung smart home ecosystems.

✔ **Example:** AI can adjust lighting, set reminders, and play music on voice command.

AI for Smart Home Security

AI-driven security systems enhance safety with real-time monitoring, facial recognition, and automated alerts.

AI Security & Surveillance Tools:

- **Ring AI & Nest Cam AI** – AI-powered video surveillance with motion detection.
- **Deep Sentinel AI** – AI-driven real-time crime prevention.
- **Vivint AI Security** – AI home monitoring with smart locks and sensors.
- **Wyze AI** – AI-powered affordable home security cameras.

✔ **Example:** AI can send real-time alerts and recognize family members vs. strangers.

AI for Energy Efficiency & Smart Climate Control

AI optimizes home energy use, reducing costs and environmental impact.

AI Smart Energy & Climate Control Devices:

- **Nest Learning Thermostat** – AI adjusts temperature based on habits.
- **EcoBee AI** – AI-powered thermostat that optimizes heating/cooling.
- **Sense AI Energy Monitor** – AI tracks energy usage and recommends savings.
- **Philips Hue AI** – AI-powered smart lighting automation.

✔ **Example:** AI can adjust heating/cooling based on weather patterns and occupancy.

AI for Smart Kitchens & Automated Cooking

AI-driven kitchen tools simplify cooking, automate meal planning, and reduce waste.

AI Kitchen & Cooking Tools:

- **June Oven AI** – AI-powered smart oven with automatic cooking settings.
- **NutriBullet Balance AI** – AI-powered blender with nutritional tracking.
- **Samsung Family Hub AI** – AI smart fridge with grocery tracking.
- **Tovala Smart Oven AI** – AI-powered meal recognition and cooking automation.

✔ **Example:** AI can suggest recipes based on available ingredients and cook food to perfection.

AI for Household Chores & Automation

AI-powered appliances automate cleaning, laundry, and household maintenance.

AI Household Automation Devices:

- **Roomba AI** – AI-powered robotic vacuum with smart mapping.
- **Braava Jet AI** – AI mop for automatic floor cleaning.
- **Litter-Robot AI** – AI-powered self-cleaning litter box.
- **Miele AI Dishwasher** – AI-powered dishwashing for optimized water usage.

✔ **Example:** AI can schedule cleaning routines and adjust to high-traffic areas in the home.

AI for Home Entertainment & Smart Living

AI enhances home entertainment with personalized recommendations and automation.

AI Entertainment & Home Theater Tools:

- **Spotify AI DJ** – AI-powered music curation.

- **Netflix & YouTube AI** – AI-driven content recommendations.
- **Sonos AI** – AI-enhanced smart speakers for premium audio.
- **LG AI ThinQ TVs** – AI-powered smart TV controls.

✔ **Example:** AI can adjust lighting and audio settings for a perfect home theater experience.

AI for a Smarter Home

AI-powered home automation enhances security, energy efficiency, convenience, and entertainment. By integrating AI into daily routines, homeowners can save time, reduce costs, and enjoy a more comfortable and connected lifestyle.

Chapter 4

AI for Financial Management & Investing

AI is revolutionizing the way we budget, save, invest, and grow wealth. With AI-powered tools, individuals can make smarter financial decisions, automate money management, and optimize investments without needing expert knowledge. AI can help you take control of your finances with ease.

AI for Budgeting & Expense Tracking

✔ **How AI Helps:**
◼ Automatically categorizes expenses and detects overspending.
◼ Creates **customized budgets** based on income and financial goals.
◼ Provides spending insights, helping you make **better financial decisions.**

AI Budgeting Tools:

- **YNAB (You Need A Budget)** – AI-driven budgeting that focuses on financial goals.
- **Mint AI** – Tracks spending and categorizes expenses automatically.
- **Cleo AI** – AI chatbot that helps manage money with spending insights and savings tips.
- **Rocket Money (formerly Truebill)** – AI that cancels unwanted subscriptions and negotiates bills.
- **PocketGuard AI** – AI-driven spending insights and bill tracking.
- **Wally AI** – AI-powered personal finance management.
- **Emma** – AI financial assistant that detects wasteful subscriptions and suggests savings

✔ **Example:** AI can predict upcoming expenses and suggest ways to save money based on spending patterns.

AI for Smart Saving, Spending & Passive Income

AI can help build automatic saving habits with setting goals, automating deposits and optimizing financial planning and creating passive income streams.

AI Savings & Passive Income Tools:

- **Digit AI** – AI-based automatic savings app that transfers money based on income and spending.

- **Acorns** – AI-driven micro-investing that rounds up spare change for investments.
- **Chime AI** – AI-assisted banking with automatic savings features.
- **Betterment** – AI-powered investing with smart portfolio management.
- **Qapital AI** – AI-powered savings automation based on spending patterns.
- **Albert AI** – AI-enhanced financial planning and emergency fund building.
- **Cleo AI** – AI-powered budgeting chatbot with savings tips.
- **Tally** – AI debt manager that helps optimize credit card payments.

✔ **Example:** AI can automatically move extra money into savings without affecting your daily spending.

AI Passive Income Strategies

AI doesn't just help with managing money—it can also help you earn more through smart automation. The AI tools can be used to create automated income generation through investing, content creation, and financial optimization.

- **AI-Generated Books & Courses** – Use AI tools to create and sell content.
- **AI Stock Trading Bots** – Automate stock or crypto investments.

- **AI Dropshipping & E-commerce** – AI-powered store management.
- **AI-Powered YouTube & Blogging** – Automate content creation for monetization.

✔ **Example:** AI can write an eBook, automate stock investments, and manage an online store—all generating passive income.

AI for Print-on-Demand & Merchandise Design

AI tools help generate unique designs for clothing, mugs, and other merchandise.

AI Print-on-Demand Design Tools:

- **Printify AI** – AI-powered product customization and fulfillment.
- **Kittl AI** – AI-enhanced typography and illustration design.
- **Mid Journey AI** – AI-generated artwork for merchandise.
- **Vexels AI** – AI-powered design templates for print-on-demand.

✔ **Example:** AI can create t-shirt designs, optimize print quality, and suggest trending styles for e-commerce.

AI Financial Advisor Tools:

AI chatbots and advisors offer customized financial insights and investment coaching.

- **Wealthsimple AI** – AI-powered financial planning and investment guidance.
- **Ellevest AI** – AI-driven investment strategies for women.
- **Kasisto AI** – AI-enhanced virtual financial assistant for banks.
- **Max AI** – AI-powered tax optimization and financial advice.

AI Retirement & Financial Planning Tools:

- **Personal Capital AI** – AI-powered retirement and wealth management.
- **NewRetirement AI** – AI-driven financial planning for retirement.
- **Savology AI** – AI-enhanced personalized financial plans.
- **Trove AI** – AI-powered investment tracking and goal planning.

✔ **Example:** AI can calculate how much you need to retire and suggest investment options.

AI for Smart Investing & Wealth Building

AI can analyze financial trends, predict market movements, risk levels and automate investment strategies.

AI Investment Platforms:

- **Wealthfront** – AI-powered investment management with tax optimization.
- **E*TRADE & TD Ameritrade AI** – AI-assisted stock trading insights.
- **Zacks AI** – AI-driven stock research and investment analysis.
- **Magnifi AI** – AI that provides stock market insights and investment recommendations.
- **Betterment AI** – AI-driven robo-advisor for hands-off investing..
- **Zignaly AI** – AI-powered cryptocurrency trading and investing signals.
- **Trade Ideas AI** – AI-driven stock market analysis and trading insights.
- **Robinhood AI** – AI-driven stock recommendations and portfolio analysis.
- **CryptoHopper AI** – AI-enhanced cryptocurrency trading automation.
- **eToro AI** – AI-powered social trading and investment strategies.
- **Napbots AI** – AI-enhanced crypto investment strategies.
- **Coinrule AI** – AI-powered custom trading rules for crypto investors.
- **Pionex AI** – AI-powered crypto trading automation.

- **Yahoo Finance AI Assistant** – AI market analysis and investment insights.

✔ **How AI Helps:**
■ Suggests **investment strategies based on risk level** and goals.
■ Identifies **stocks, ETFs, and cryptocurrency trends.**
■ Automated **portfolio balancing** to maximize returns.

AI for Credit & Debt Management

AI can optimize credit scores, reduce debt, and help manage loans effectively.

AI Credit & Debt Management Tools:

- **Experian Boost AI** – Uses AI to improve credit scores with positive payment history.
- **Tally AI** – AI-driven debt repayment strategy tool.
- **Credit Karma AI** – AI-powered credit monitoring and loan recommendations.
- **Upstart AI** – AI-backed personal loan approval based on future earning potential.
- **Rocket Money AI** – AI-powered subscription management and bill negotiation.

✔ **Example:** AI can suggest personalized repayment plans to reduce interest and get out of debt faster

AI for Fraud Detection & Financial Security

AI can protect your finances by detecting fraudulent transactions and improving security.

AI Fraud Detection & Security Tools:

- **Plaid AI** – AI-secured banking and identity verification.
- **FICO Falcon Fraud Manager** – AI-driven fraud prevention for banking.
- **Aura AI** – AI-powered identity theft protection.
- **Chase AI Security** – AI that detects and prevents fraud in banking transactions.
- **Experian AI** – AI-powered identity theft protection and credit monitoring.
- **Chime AI** – AI-enhanced fraud alerts and account security.
- **IBM Watson AI for Fraud Detection** – AI-driven risk assessment for financial transactions.
- **PayPal AI** – AI-powered fraud protection and purchase security.
- **Darktrace AI** – AI-driven cybersecurity for financial protection.
- **Kount AI** – AI-enhanced fraud prevention for digital transactions.
- **ID.me AI** – AI-powered identity verification and security.

✔ **Example:** AI can monitor accounts in real time, flagging suspicious activity before it becomes a financial loss.

AI as Your Financial Assistant

AI makes budgeting, saving, investing, and financial security easier and more efficient. Whether you're looking to manage daily expenses, grow your wealth, or secure your finances, AI can provide personalized insights and automation to help you achieve financial success.

Chapter 5

AI for Communication & Relationships

AI is transforming the way we connect, communicate, and build relationships. Whether you're improving social skills, maintaining long-distance relationships, or enhancing workplace communication, AI can help foster stronger, more meaningful connections.

AI for Dating & Finding Love

AI-powered dating apps use machine learning and behavioral analysis to match people based on compatibility.

AI Dating & Matchmaking Tools:

- **Tinder AI** – AI-enhanced matching based on swiping patterns.

- **Hinge AI** – AI-powered compatibility scoring and conversation starters.
- **eHarmony AI** – AI-driven personality-based matchmaking.
- **Iris AI** – AI-powered face recognition for ideal matches.

✔ **Example:** AI can analyze past interactions and suggest better matches based on personality compatibility.

AI for Language Translation & Cross-Cultural Communication

AI can break language barriers, making global communication faster and more accurate.

AI Translation Tools:

- **Google Translate** – AI-powered text, speech, and image translation.
- **DeepL** – Advanced AI language translation for professionals.
- **iTranslate & SayHi** – AI-based voice translation apps.

✔ **Example:** AI can translate messages in real time, helping businesses and travelers communicate effortlessly.

AI Social Skills Tools:

- **Grammarly AI** – AI-enhanced writing and communication suggestions.
- **Orai AI** – AI-powered speech coaching and public speaking.
- **QuillBot AI** – AI-driven paraphrasing and conversation improvement.
- **Social Q AI** – AI-enhanced social skill development and confidence building.

✔ **Example:** AI can suggest better ways to phrase messages, helping users avoid misunderstandings.

AI for Relationship Building & Social Skills

AI-powered tools can improve social interactions, dating experiences, and emotional intelligence.

AI Social & Relationship Tools:

- **Replika** – AI companion for social and emotional connection.
- **QuillBot** – AI-enhanced conversation and writing assistance.
- **Hily & eHarmony AI Matching** – AI-driven dating apps that suggest compatible matches.
- **Love Nudge AI** – AI-enhanced love language coaching.
- **Talkspace AI** – AI-driven couples therapy and counseling.

- **Pillow Talk AI** – AI-powered long-distance relationship support.

✔ **How AI Helps:**

■ Suggests **better ways to express emotions** and communicate effectively.

■ Provides **AI-generated conversation starters** for dating and networking.

■ Analyzes **tone in messages** to improve clarity and emotional impact.

AI Friendship & Social Planning Tools:

AI tools can help maintain friendships by sending reminders, suggesting activities, and improving social interactions which can expand professional circles as well.

- **Google Assistant AI** – AI-powered reminders for birthdays and events.
- **We3 AI** – AI-driven friend-matching for social networking.
- **Bumble BFF AI** – AI-powered friendship matching.
- **Meetup AI** – AI-enhanced event and activity suggestions.
- **Evite AI** – AI-powered event invitations and RSVPs.
- **Doodle AI** – AI-enhanced scheduling and group coordination.
- **Bizzabo AI** – AI-driven event marketing and management.

AI Networking Tools:

- **LinkedIn AI** – AI-enhanced professional networking and job matching.
- **Lunchclub AI** – AI-powered networking for career growth.
- **Shapr AI** – AI-driven professional matchmaking.
- **Clubhouse AI** – AI-enhanced voice-based networking.

✔ **Example:** AI can remind you to check in with friends and suggest fun activities based on shared interests.

AI Long-Distance Relationship Tools:

- **Kast AI** – AI-enhanced virtual movie nights and co-watching experiences.
- **HeyTell AI** – AI-powered voice messaging for instant connection.
- **Bond Touch AI** – AI-driven touch communication devices.
- **Lovense AI** – AI-enhanced intimacy tools for long-distance couples.

✔ **Example:** AI can suggest virtual date ideas and enhance real-time communication.

AI for Emotional Intelligence & Conflict Resolution

AI can help analyze conversations, detect emotions, and provide guidance on resolving conflicts.

AI Emotional & Conflict Resolution Tools:

- **Ellie AI** – AI chatbot for emotional intelligence training.
- **Crystal Knows** – AI personality analysis for better communication.
- **Wysa** – AI-powered emotional support chatbot.
- **Woebot AI** – AI-driven emotional support and conflict guidance.
- **Mood AI** – AI-powered mood tracking for emotional awareness.
- **EQ Chat AI** – AI-enhanced emotional intelligence training.
- **Relate AI** – AI-powered relationship analytics

✔ **How AI Helps:**

■ Detects **emotions in conversations** and suggests thoughtful responses.

■ Helps **resolve workplace or personal conflicts** with AI-driven guidance.

■ Improves **self-awareness and empathy** in communication.

AI as a Communication Enhancer

AI is revolutionizing the way we interact, making communication more effective, inclusive, and emotionally intelligent. Whether it's for personal relationships, workplace collaboration, or cross-cultural connections, AI provides support in bridging the gaps, strengthening human interactions and building meaningful relationships.

Chapter 6

AI for Learning

AI is revolutionizing education by making learning more personalized, accessible, and efficient. From AI tutors to automated grading, AI enhances student engagement, skill development, and academic success.

AI for Personalized Study Plans & Time Management

AI tools help students and professionals organize their schedules and optimize study habits.

AI Study & Time Management Tools:

- **Notion AI** – AI-powered note-taking and task organization.
- **Forest AI** – AI-driven focus and productivity tracking.
- **Evernote AI** – AI-enhanced digital note organization.
- **Todoist AI** – AI-powered study and task management.

✔ **Example:** AI can create customized study schedules, track deadlines, and suggest break intervals for better focus.

AI-Powered Personalized Learning

AI customizes learning experiences based on individual needs, strengths, and weaknesses.

AI Learning Platforms:

- **Khan Academy's Khanmigo AI** – AI-powered tutor for personalized learning.
- **Socratic by Google AI** – AI-driven homework helper and explainer.
- **Coursera AI & Udemy AI** – AI-enhanced course recommendations and skill tracking.
- **Edmentum Exact Path AI** – AI-driven K-12 personalized learning tool.
- **Quizlet AI** – AI-generated flashcards and personalized study plans.
- **Duolingo AI** – AI-enhanced language learning with adaptive exercises.
- **Curiosity AI** – AI-powered knowledge discovery.
- **MasterClass AI** – AI-enhanced learning from industry experts.
- **Brilliant AI** – AI-driven problem-solving and logic development.

✔ **Example:** AI can identify knowledge gaps and suggest tailored lessons based on your learning speed and understanding.

AI for Reading & Comprehension

AI-powered tools improve reading speed, comprehension, and content summarization.

AI Reading Tools:

- **Blinkist AI** – AI-driven book summaries.
- **Speechify AI** – AI-powered text-to-speech for audio learning.
- **Readwise AI** – AI-enhanced reading highlights and retention.
- **Scribd AI** – AI-driven personalized book recommendations.

✔ **Example:** AI can summarize long articles and highlight key takeaways for faster learning.

AI for Interactive & Gamified Learning

AI-driven gamification makes learning fun and engaging.

AI Gamified Learning Tools:

- **Prodigy AI** – AI-powered math learning through games.

- **Brainscape AI** – AI-enhanced flashcard-based learning.
- **Kahoot AI** – AI-driven interactive quizzes and games.
- **Duolingo AI** – AI-powered gamified language learning.

✔ **Example:** AI can turn complex subjects into engaging quizzes and interactive challenges to boost retention.

AI for Homework Help & Tutoring

AI-powered tutors provide instant explanations, step-by-step solutions, and interactive learning. It also supports teachers by automating grading, generating lesson plans, and engaging students.

AI Homework & Tutoring Tools:

- **ChatGPT AI Tutor** – AI-powered tutor for various subjects.
- **Photomath AI** – AI-driven step-by-step math problem solver.
- **Brainly AI** – AI-powered student Q&A platform.
- **Quillbot AI** – AI-powered writing assistant for grammar and paraphrasing.
- **Elicit AI** – AI-driven research paper summarization.
- **Wolfram Alpha AI** – AI-powered math problem-solving and data analysis.
- **Perplexity AI** – AI-enhanced fact-checking and knowledge retrieval.

- **Otter.ai** – AI-powered lecture transcription and note-taking.
- **Khan Academy AI (Khanmigo)** – AI-powered virtual tutoring

✔ **Example:** AI can explain complex concepts in a simplified, engaging way and also help with citations for research papers. What a relief!

AI for Test Preparation & Exam Success

AI-powered test prep tools help students practice, analyze mistakes, and improve test scores.

AI Test Prep Tools:

- **Magoosh AI** – AI-enhanced SAT, GRE, and GMAT prep.
- **PrepScholar AI** – AI-powered personalized test study plans.
- **UWorld AI** – AI-driven MCAT, USMLE, and nursing exam practice.
- **Anki AI** – AI-generated flashcards for exam memorization.
- **Albert AI** – AI-driven practice questions for AP exams and more.

✔ **Example:** AI can analyze past test performance, predict weak areas, and suggest targeted practice questions.

AI for Speed Reading & Summarizing Information

Reading long articles or research papers can take time, but AI can help you summarize, highlight key points, and generate insights in seconds.

AI Summarization Tools:

- **TLDRThis** – Summarizes articles and PDFs.
- **QuillBot** – AI paraphrasing and summarizing tool.
- **Claude AI** – Uploads and analyzes large documents for key takeaways.

✔ **Example:** Upload a 50-page whitepaper and ask AI to extract the 5 most important points.

AI for Skill Development & Career Training

AI helps learners develop new skills and advance their careers with tailored course recommendations.

AI Skill & Career Training Platforms:

- **LinkedIn Learning AI** – AI-driven career development courses.
- **Skillshare AI** – AI-powered personalized course suggestions.
- **Udacity AI & Codecademy AI** – AI-driven coding and tech skill-building.

- **Google Grow with AI** – AI-powered career growth and certification programs.
- **Coursera AI** – AI-enhanced personalized course recommendations.
- **Udemy AI** – AI-driven skill development tutorials.

✔ **Example:** AI can suggest relevant skills and courses based on industry trends along with recommending the best online courses and provide interactive exercises tailored to your career goals.

AI for Language Learning

AI-powered language tools enhance translation, pronunciation, and fluency.

AI Language Learning Tools:

- **Duolingo AI** – AI-powered language learning with personalized practice.
- **Google Translate AI** – AI-driven instant text and speech translation.
- **ChatGPT AI for Language Practice** – AI conversation partner for language learners.
- **Elsa Speak AI** – AI-powered pronunciation and accent training.
- **LingQ AI** – AI-powered reading and vocabulary learning.
- **Rosetta Stone AI** – AI-powered speech recognition for pronunciation.

✔ **Example:** AI can simulate real-world conversations and provide instant feedback.

AI for Writing & Research Assistance

AI-powered writing assistants help with essay writing, grammar, and research organization.

How to Use AI for Research:

1. Ask AI for a **summary** of a complex topic.
   - *Example:* "Summarize the key benefits of AI in healthcare."
2. Have AI **compare different viewpoints** on a topic.
   - *Example:* "What are the pros and cons of AI in education?"
3. Use AI to **fact-check and find sources** by asking, "What are reliable sources for [topic]?"

✔ **Pro Tip: ALWAYS** double-check AI-generated research with credible sources before publishing or making decisions.

AI Writing & Research Tools:

- **Grammarly AI** – AI-powered grammar and style checker.
- **Hemingway Editor AI** – AI-enhanced readability and writing improvement.

- **Zotero AI & Mendeley AI** – AI-driven research and citation management.
- **ChatGPT & Perplexity AI** – Answer questions, summarize articles, and generate research reports.
- **Jasper AI** – AI-driven essay and content generation.
- **Quillbot AI** – AI-powered paraphrasing and summarization.
- **Elicit AI** – AI-powered academic research assistant.
- **Google Scholar + Semantic Scholar** – AI-driven academic search engines.

✔ **Example:** AI can help structure essays, generate ideas, and proofread content.

AI for Educational Accessibility

AI-powered tools support students with disabilities and different learning needs.

AI Accessibility Tools:

- **Speechify AI & NaturalReader AI** – AI-powered text-to-speech for reading assistance.
- **Be My Eyes AI** – AI-driven assistance for visually impaired users.
- **Otter.ai & Rev AI** – AI-powered transcription and note-taking.
- **Microsoft Immersive Reader AI** – AI-enhanced reading comprehension tool.

- **Ghotit AI** – AI-powered dyslexia-friendly writing assistance.
- **Dragon NaturallySpeaking AI** – AI-enhanced speech-to-text technology.
- **Seeing AI** – AI-powered vision assistance for visually impaired learners.

✔ **Example:** AI can read aloud texts, provide subtitles, and assist visually impaired learners.

AI for Automated Grading & Feedback

AI streamlines grading, assessments, and instant feedback helping teachers.

AI Grading & Assessment Tools:

- **Gradescope AI** – AI-powered automated grading for teachers.
- **Turnitin AI** – AI-driven plagiarism detection and writing feedback.
- **Quillionz AI** – AI-generated quizzes and test questions.
- **Knewton AI** – AI-powered adaptive assessments for students.
- **ScribeSense AI** – AI-driven automated grading.
- **Google Classroom AI** – AI-enhanced education management.

✔ **Example:** AI can evaluate assignments and provide instant feedback, saving teachers time.

AI as the Future of Learning

AI is reshaping education by making learning more interactive, personalized, efficient, and accessible. Whether you're a student, teacher or life long learner, AI powered tools can help you gain knowledge faster, stay organized, and develop new skills efficiently.

Chapter 7

AI for Creativity & Content Creation

So many artists can go through bouts of "writer's block" where it feels like the page in front of you will be blank forever. Writing is one of the most time-consuming tasks, whether it's emails, blogs, books, or social media content. AI has rapidly become a tool for writers of all kinds as it can assist with brainstorming, drafting, editing, and even generating ideas, making content creation faster, easier and less stressful by enhancing creativity without replacing human imagination.

AI for Writing & Content Generation

AI-powered tools assist with blog posts, stories, books, poetry, scripts, social media content, and copywriting.

AI Writing Tools:

- **ChatGPT AI** – AI-powered content creation, brainstorming, and editing.
- **Jasper AI** – AI-driven marketing copy and blog writing assistant.
- **Copy.ai & Writesonic AI** – AI-generated ad copy, social media posts, and SEO content.
- **Sudowrite AI** – AI-powered creative writing tool for novelists and storytellers.

✔ **Example:** AI can generate article outlines, rewrite content, and enhance storytelling.

How to Use AI for Writing:

1. **Ask AI for an outline** – "Give me an outline for a blog about AI side hustles."
2. **Generate a rough draft** – "Write an introduction on how AI helps content creators."
3. **Refine & edit** – Use AI suggestions, then rewrite in your voice.

Ever thought about writing a book? Neither did I, until I found out how easy it is with AI. Literally from the beginning, AI can help you with every step. Not sure what to write about? AI will give you ideas based on keywords or prompts that will help you discover new angles and perspectives. How about the fact that it can even help you develop characters by creating profiles, backstories and even dialogue all while following the story outline and suggesting plot twists. It can draft it all up and then you just gotta look it over to see if you want to put your own twist on it and of course you should always do your research and make sure there is no plagiarism. Need a reference page for a non-fiction book, no problem. With information summarization to save you time and fact checking to ensure accuracy, AI can do all the difficult work for you.

Using AI for Editing & Proofreading

AI doesn't just help you write—it also fixes grammar, improves clarity, and makes writing stronger.

While having the use of spelling being corrected on Word for quite some time now, using AI to help reword a sentence or two is so amazing. Your work will flow better and you won't get stuck rephrasing over and over trying to get it right.

As an example, I just asked AI to rephrase the above paragraph. Here are two options it gave me:

- "Beyond the familiar spell check, AI's ability to refine sentences is a game changer, enhancing writing flow and eliminating frustrating rewrites."
- "We've relied on spell check for years, but AI now offers a powerful edge: instant sentence refinement that boosts writing flow and saves you from endless rephrasing."

Both of those definitely sound better than the first. AI gave me many options along with what tone I wanted it to have, whether that be more concise or more conversational. The refinement is endless.

AI Editing Tools:

✔ Use these tools to **polish** AI-generated content before publishing.

- **Grammarly** – Corrects grammar & suggests better phrasing.
- **ProWritingAid** – Detailed style & grammar check.
- **Hemingway Editor** – Simplifies complex sentences for better readability.

AI for Digital Art & Design

AI helps artists **create, enhance, and modify artwork with advanced generative models.**

Want to add eye-catching visuals to your content? Unleash visual creativity with AI. Generate unique images for any project, from blog posts to book covers. Ditch searching for stock photos that cost you money. Inspire your writing by prompting AI to bring your characters and scenes to life, with no design skills needed.

AI Art & Design Tools:

- **Canva AI** – AI-powered graphic design and content creation.

- **Adobe Firefly AI** – AI-enhanced image generation and editing.
- **Deep Dream AI** AI-powered creative and surreal digital art.
- **DALL·E AI & MidJourney AI** – AI-generated artwork from text prompts.
- **Runway AI** – AI-driven video and image creation.

✔ **Example:** AI can turn simple sketches into detailed digital prints, generate concept art, create logos, and design digital illustrations.

AI for Animation & 3D Modeling

AI animation tools help generate characters, animate scenes, and create 3D models.

AI Animation & 3D Tools:

- **Blender AI Add-ons** – AI-powered 3D modeling enhancements.
- **DeepMotion AI** – AI-driven motion capture for animation.
- **Daz 3D AI** – AI-enhanced character creation.
- **Plask AI** – AI-powered motion tracking and animation.

✔ **Example:** AI can generate animated characters, create 3D assets, and automate facial expressions in animation.

AI for Photography & Image Enhancement

AI-powered tools edit photos, restore images, and enhance visual quality.

AI Photography & Editing Tools:

- **Luminar AI** – AI-powered photo editing and retouching.
- **Topaz AI** – AI-enhanced image sharpening and noise reduction.
- **Remove.bg AI** – AI-driven background removal.
- **Fotor AI** – AI-powered image enhancement and effects.

✔ **Example:** AI can automatically enhance images, remove backgrounds, and create professional-quality visuals.

AI for Music Composition & Audio Editing

AI tools help create original music, enhance sound quality, generate voice overs and edit audio tracks.

AI Music & Audio Tools:

- **AIVA AI** – AI-powered music composition for films and games.
- **Boomy AI** – AI-generated original music and beats.
- **LANDR AI** – AI-driven audio mastering and production.
- **Amper AI** – AI-generated background music for videos and ads.

- **LALAL.AI** – AI-enhanced audio separation and noise reduction.
- **Murf AI** – AI-powered voiceovers and speech synthesis.
- **ElevenLabs** – AI-generated voiceovers for audiobooks.
- **Descript** – Transcribes & edits podcast/audio content.

✔ **Example:** AI can compose background music for YouTube videos or generate unique soundtracks.

AI for Video Creation & Editing

AI enhances video production by automating editing, generating effects, and improving quality.

AI Video Editing Tools:

- **Runway AI** – AI-powered video editing and motion graphics.
- **Synthesia AI** – AI-generated video content with virtual presenters.
- **Descript AI** – AI-powered video editing, captioning, and voiceovers.
- **Pictory AI** – AI-driven automatic video summarization and highlights.
- **DeepBrain AI** – AI-driven animation and visual effects
- **Lumen5** – AI video creation for YouTube & social media.

✔ **Example:** AI can automatically cut and edit footage, add captions, and generate voiceovers.

AI for Social Media Content Creation

AI streamlines content planning, scheduling, and engagement on social platforms.

AI Social Media Tools:

- **Lately AI** – AI-powered social media post generation.
- **Buffer AI** – AI-driven social media scheduling and analytics.
- **Predis AI** – AI-generated Instagram, Twitter, and Facebook posts.
- **Synthesia AI & HeyGen AI** – AI-powered talking avatar videos for social media.
- **Taplio AI** – AI-enhanced LinkedIn post generation and audience growth.
- **Brandmark AI** – AI-powered logo and branding design.
- **Hootsuite AI** – AI-powered social media scheduling and engagement tracking.
- **CapCut AI** – AI-powered video editing for social media.

✔ **Example:** AI can automate social media posting and generate engaging captions.

AI Blogging & Website Tools:

- **WordPress AI Plugins** – AI-powered SEO and content generation.
- **Frase AI** – AI-driven content optimization for blogs.

- **Writesonic AI** – AI-enhanced article writing and website content.
- **Wix AI** – AI-powered website design and customization.

✔ **Example:** AI can build a website, write blog content, and optimize SEO to attract traffic.

AI for Creative Brainstorming & Storytelling

AI helps generate fresh ideas, structure plots, and improve storytelling by overcoming creative blocks.

AI Storytelling Tools:

- **NovelAI** – AI-powered storytelling and world-building.
- **DeepStory AI** – AI-generated screenplay and storytelling assistance.
- **Shortly AI** – AI-enhanced creative writing and expansion.
- **ChatGPT AI** – AI-driven plot development and dialogue generation.
- **Rytr AI** – AI-driven brainstorming for marketing and storytelling.
- **MindMeister AI** – AI-enhanced mind mapping and idea organization.
- **StoryLab AI** – AI-powered story and script idea generation.

✔ **Example:** AI can be used to generate story ideas, build characters, and expand dialogue.

AI for Creative Collaboration & Workflow Automation

AI tools enable seamless collaboration among creative teams while automating repetitive tasks.

AI Collaboration & Workflow Tools:

- **Notion AI** – AI-powered content organization and collaboration.
- **Trello AI** – AI-enhanced project management for creative teams.
- **Otter.ai** – AI-powered transcription and note-taking for meetings.
- **Figma AI** – AI-driven design collaboration and prototyping.

✔ **Example:** AI can help creative teams organize projects, automate content planning, and improve productivity.

AI for Branding & Marketing Content

AI assists entrepreneurs, influencers, and businesses with content marketing strategies.

AI Branding & Marketing Tools:

- **Brandmark AI** – AI-powered logo and branding design.
- **Persado AI** – AI-generated persuasive marketing copy.

- **AdCreative AI** – AI-powered ad design and conversion optimization.
- **Headline AI** – AI-driven SEO and blog headline generation.

✔ **Example:** AI can help entrepreneurs create professional branding materials and marketing campaigns.

AI for Copyright & Intellectual Property Protection

AI tools help creators protect their work from plagiarism and copyright infringement.

AI Copyright & Protection Tools:

- **Copyscape AI** – AI-powered plagiarism detection for writers.
- **Pixsy AI** – AI-driven image copyright protection and infringement detection.
- **Lumen AI** – AI-enhanced legal assistance for intellectual property rights.
- **Originality.ai** – AI-powered content originality checking.

✔ **Example:** AI can scan the internet for stolen artwork or detect AI-generated plagiarism.

AI as a Creative Partner

AI art generators are incredible tools, capable of conjuring stunning visuals that can spark creativity and streamline design processes. They empower creators to explore new ideas and bring concepts to life with remarkable speed. However, it is crucial to remember that **AI is a tool, not an artist. The true mastery of artistic skill, honed through countless hours of dedicated practice in drawing, painting or sculpting (amongst many forms of art), remains uniquely human. The love, passion, and individual touch that handmade artists infuse into their work create pieces of irreplaceable value and uniqueness. While AI can assist and inspire, it should never overshadow the profound dedication and artistry of human creators.**

Chapter 8

AI for Entrepreneurship & Business Growth

AI is transforming how businesses operate, making it easier for entrepreneurs to automate tasks, optimize decision-making, improve customer service, and increase profitability. Whether you're a solopreneur, small business owner, or startup founder, AI can help you scale efficiently while reducing costs. The tool is also making it easier than ever to find jobs, optimize resumes, network, and develop new skills. AI-powered tools can help you stand out and succeed in today's competitive job market.

AI for Resume & Cover Letter Optimization

AI-powered resume tools can analyze job descriptions, highlight key skills, and improve formatting to increase your chances of getting hired.

AI Resume & Cover Letter Tools:

- **Zety AI** – AI-powered resume builder with customizable templates.
- **Resume.io AI** – AI-enhanced resume formatting and keyword optimization.
- **Kickresume AI** – AI-driven resume and cover letter generation.
- **Teal AI** – AI-powered job application tracking and resume analysis.

✔ **Example:** AI can scan job descriptions and adjust your resume to match the most relevant skills.

AI for Interview Preparation & Mock Interviews

AI-driven interview coaches analyze tone, speech patterns, and body language to help users improve their confidence.

AI Interview Prep Tools:

- **Interview Warmup AI** – AI-powered mock interview practice by Google.
- **Yoodli AI** – AI-driven speech analysis and public speaking coaching.
- **HireVue AI** – AI-enhanced video interview feedback.
- **Big Interview AI** – AI-powered interview coaching with real-time feedback.

✔ **Example:** AI can provide instant feedback on your interview answers and suggest improvements.

AI for Job Searching & Application Tracking

AI tools can match candidates with jobs based on experience, skills, and preferences, reducing the time spent searching.

AI Job Search & Application Tracking Tools:

- **LinkedIn AI** – AI-powered job recommendations and networking insights.
- **Indeed AI** – AI-enhanced job matching and resume ranking.
- **Jobscan AI** – AI-driven applicant tracking system (ATS) optimization.
- **HiredScore AI** – AI-powered candidate screening and job matching.

✔ **Example:** AI can analyze thousands of job postings and recommend the best matches based on your qualifications.

AI for Skill Development & Career Advancement

AI-powered learning platforms provide personalized courses, skill assessments, and career growth opportunities.

AI Learning & Skill Development Platforms:

- **Coursera AI** – AI-driven course recommendations and career paths.
- **Udemy AI** – AI-powered skill-building courses in various industries.
- **Skillshare AI** – AI-enhanced creative and professional development courses.
- **LinkedIn Learning AI** – AI-powered career training and certifications.

✔ **Example:** AI can recommend the best courses to help you transition into a higher-paying job.

AI for Freelancers & Gig Workers

AI helps freelancers find high-paying gigs, optimize portfolios, and automate workflows.

AI Tools for Freelancers:

- **Fiverr AI** – AI-powered gig recommendations and pricing strategies.
- **Upwork AI** – AI-driven job matching for freelancers.
- **Jasper AI** – AI-enhanced content creation and copywriting.
- **Canva AI** – AI-powered graphic design assistance.

✔ **Example:** AI can help you find freelance opportunities that match your skills and experience.

AI for Business Automation

AI-powered automation tools save time by handling repetitive tasks, improving efficiency, and streamlining workflows.

AI Automation Tools:

- **Zapier AI** – Automates workflows between apps and services.
- **IFTTT AI** – Connects different apps to automate tasks.
- **Bardeen AI** – AI-powered browser automation for data entry and web tasks.
- **UiPath AI** – Advanced robotic process automation (RPA) for businesses.
- **Notion AI** – AI-driven workflow and productivity assistant.
- **Trello AI** – AI-enhanced project management.
- **Airtable AI** – AI-powered database and business organization.

✔ **Example:** AI can automatically update customer data, send emails, and schedule social media posts.

AI Workplace Productivity Tools:

- **Grammarly AI** – AI-powered writing and editing assistance.
- **Notion AI** – AI-enhanced note-taking and organization.
- **Trello AI** – AI-powered task management and team collaboration.

- **Clockify AI** – AI-driven time tracking and efficiency insights.

✔ **Example:** AI can automate meeting notes, schedule tasks, and boost workplace efficiency.

AI for Hiring & Team Collaboration

AI recruiting and HR tools streamline hiring, analyze resumes, and improve team communication.

AI Hiring & Team Management Tools:

- **HireVue AI** – AI-powered candidate screening.
- **Recruitee AI** – AI-driven hiring automation.
- **Slack AI** – AI-enhanced team collaboration.
- **Monday.com AI** – AI-powered project management.

✔ **Example:** AI can screen job applicants, schedule interviews, and match candidates to roles.

AI for Customer Service & Chatbots

AI chatbots provide 24/7 customer support, handle inquiries, and boost engagement.

AI Chatbot & Customer Support Tools:

- **ChatGPT AI for Business** – AI-powered customer interaction and support.
- **Drift AI** – AI-driven chatbot for customer engagement and lead generation.
- **Tidio AI** – AI chatbot for e-commerce customer service.
- **Zendesk AI** – AI-powered support ticketing and chatbot automation.
- **Intercom AI** – AI-enhanced customer engagement.

✔ **Example:** AI can answer common customer questions and direct users to the right resources.

AI for Marketing & Growth Strategies

AI-driven marketing tools help analyze trends, generate ads,improve audience targeting and optimize campaigns.

AI Marketing & Advertising Tools:

- **HubSpot AI** – AI-powered marketing, sales, and CRM automation.
- **Persado AI** – AI-generated persuasive marketing copy.
- **AdCreative AI** – AI-driven ad design and conversion optimization.
- **Surfer SEO AI** – AI-powered SEO content strategy tool.
- **Jasper AI** – AI-powered content creation and copywriting.
- **Copy.ai** – AI-driven marketing copy and email writing.

- **Adzooma AI** – AI-enhanced Google and Facebook ad optimization.
- **Persado AI** – AI-powered emotional marketing content

✔ **Example:** AI can generate high-converting ad copy and optimize email marketing campaigns and generate blog posts.

AI for Market Research & Competitive Analysis

AI-powered analytics help businesses stay ahead of industry trends and competitors.

AI Market Research Tools:

- **SimilarWeb AI** – AI-driven competitor analysis.
- **SEMrush AI** – AI-powered keyword and market research.
- **Crayon AI** – AI-enhanced business intelligence.
- **BuzzSumo AI** – AI-driven content trend analysis.

✔ **Example:** AI can analyze competitor strategies and suggest improvements to outperform them.

AI for Lead Generation & Sales Growth

AI optimizes sales outreach, customer targeting, and lead conversion.

AI Lead Generation Tools:

- **HubSpot AI** – AI-powered CRM and lead tracking.
- **Apollo AI** – AI-enhanced email prospecting.
- **Seamless AI** – AI-driven sales lead discovery.
- **Clearbit AI** – AI-powered customer insights.

✔ **Example:** AI can identify potential customers and suggest personalized outreach strategies.

AI for Financial Management & Bookkeeping

AI helps manage finances by tracking expenses, analyzing cash flow, and detecting fraud.

AI Finance & Accounting Tools:

- **QuickBooks AI** – AI-powered bookkeeping and financial tracking.
- **Fyle AI** – AI-driven expense management and receipt tracking.
- **Vic.ai** – AI-powered accounts payable automation.
- **Tesorio AI** – AI-driven cash flow forecasting and financial planning.
- **Xero AI** – AI-enhanced financial tracking.
- **Penny AI** – AI-powered sales and revenue forecasting.
- **Fathom AI** – AI-driven financial analytics for businesses.
- **LivePlan AI** – AI-driven business plan creation.

✔ Example: AI can categorize transactions, generate financial reports, and automate invoicing.

AI for Salary Negotiation & Career Growth

AI-powered platforms help professionals evaluate salaries, negotiate pay raises, and plan career moves.

AI Salary & Career Growth Tools:

- **Payscale AI** – AI-driven salary comparisons and negotiation insights.
- **Glassdoor AI** – AI-enhanced salary benchmarking and job reviews.
- **Levels.fyi AI** – AI-powered compensation insights for tech careers.
- **Pathrise AI** – AI-driven career mentorship and salary negotiation strategies.

✔ Example: AI can analyze salary trends and suggest the best negotiation tactics for your industry.

AI for Product Development & E-commerce

AI helps identify trends, optimize pricing, and improve customer experience.

AI E-commerce & Product Development Tools:

- **Shopify AI** – AI-driven store optimization and customer insights.
- **Printify AI & Printful AI** – AI-powered print-on-demand product design.
- **Vue.ai** – AI-generated personalized shopping experiences.
- **Algolia AI** – AI-powered search and product recommendations.
- **Sell The Trend AI** – AI-enhanced product research for dropshipping.
- **Chatfuel AI** – AI-powered sales chatbots for e-commerce.
- **Sellbrite AI** – AI-powered multi-channel selling.
- **Adzooma AI** – AI-optimized e-commerce advertising.

✔ **Example:** AI can analyze customer preferences to suggest personalized product recommendations, find trending products, create product descriptions, and automate store operations.

AI for Business Intelligence & Decision-Making

AI helps business owners make data-driven decisions with predictive analytics and trend analysis.

AI Business Intelligence Tools:

- **Tableau AI** – AI-powered data visualization and insights.
- **Microsoft Power BI AI** – AI-driven business analytics.
- **MonkeyLearn AI** – AI-powered sentiment analysis and market research.

- **Google Analytics AI** – AI-driven website traffic and customer behavior analysis.
- **Looker AI** – AI-driven data analytics.
- **Klipfolio AI** – AI-enhanced business performance tracking.
- **IBM Watson AI** – AI-powered data-driven decision-making.

✔ **Example:** AI can predict future sales trends based on customer behavior.

AI for Content Creation & Branding

AI enhances branding, logo design, and content marketing faster and more efficiently.

AI Branding & Networking Tools:

- **Brandmark AI** – AI-generated logos and branding materials.
- **Lumen5 AI** – AI-powered video creation for branding and marketing.
- **Jasper AI** – AI-generated content for blogs and ads.
- **Grammarly AI** – AI-enhanced business writing and communication.
- **Copy.ai** – AI-enhanced marketing copy generation.
- **Surfer SEO AI** – AI-driven content optimization.
- **Synthesia AI** – AI-powered video content creation.

✔ **Example:** AI can help businesses generate consistent branding and content marketing strategies by writing social media captions, email campaigns, and blog posts in seconds.

AI Social Media Management Tools:

- **Crystal AI** – AI-powered personality insights for better networking.
- **Taplio AI** – AI-enhanced LinkedIn post generation and profile optimization.
- **Hootsuite AI** – AI-powered social media growth and engagement tracking.
- **Canva AI** – AI-driven personal branding and portfolio creation.
- **Lately AI** – AI-driven content repurposing for social media.
- **Buffer AI** – AI-enhanced social media automation.
- **Pictory AI** – AI-driven video creation for social media.

✔ **Example:** AI can auto-generate engaging posts and suggest the best times to publish for maximum reach through analyzed data.

AI for Legal & Contract Management

AI tools assist with legal document generation, contract management, and compliance.

AI Legal Tools:

- **DoNotPay AI** – AI-powered legal assistance and contract negotiation.
- **LawGeex AI** – AI-driven contract review and compliance.
- **Lex Machina AI** – AI-powered legal analytics for businesses.
- **Juro AI** – AI-generated contract automation and management.
- **LegalZoom AI** – AI-enhanced business formation and compliance.
- **DocuSign AI** – AI-driven digital contracts.
- **TrademarkNow AI** – AI-powered trademark protection.

✔ **Example:** AI can draft standard contracts, review legal agreements, and detect compliance risks.

AI as a Business Growth Engine & Career Coach

AI is transforming the way people approach job searching, networking, and career development by offering personalized insights, streamlining applications, and enhancing workplace productivity. With the help of AI-driven tools, professionals can uncover better opportunities, grow their skills, and advance toward long-term career goals.

For entrepreneurs, AI is reshaping how businesses operate — from automating daily tasks and improving customer interactions to supporting smarter decision-making. These tools enable businesses to grow faster, cut costs, and work more efficiently

Chapter 9

AI for Travel & Transportation

AI is revolutionizing how we plan, book, and experience travel, making trips more efficient, affordable, and enjoyable. From AI-driven trip planning to self-driving cars, AI enhances convenience, safety, and personalization in transportation.

AI-Powered Travel Planning & Booking

AI simplifies travel planning by analyzing preferences, suggesting itineraries, and finding the best deals.

AI Travel Planning Tools:

- **Google Travel AI** – AI-powered flight tracking, hotel booking, and itinerary organization.

- **Hopper AI** – Predicts the best time to book flights & hotels for lower prices.
- **Expedia AI & Kayak AI** – AI-driven travel search engines for personalized recommendations.
- **TripIt AI** – AI travel assistant that organizes itineraries and alerts for changes.

✔ **Example:** AI can analyze past trips and preferences to suggest personalized travel plans.

AI for Flight & Hotel Recommendations

AI finds the best flight and hotel options based on pricing, amenities, and reviews.

AI Flight & Hotel Search Tools:

- **Skyscanner AI** – AI-powered flight and hotel deal predictions.
- **Trivago AI & Priceline AI** – AI-driven hotel comparison tools.
- **Google Flights AI** – AI-powered flight price tracking and alerts.
- **Hotel Tonight AI** – AI-powered last-minute hotel deals.

✔ **Example:** AI can track flight price trends and notify travelers when prices drop.

AI-Powered Virtual Travel Assistants

AI chatbots and virtual assistants help travelers with real-time information and booking support.

AI Travel Assistants:

- **Lola AI** – AI-powered travel concierge for booking and itinerary changes.
- **Mezi AI (by American Express)** – AI chatbot for travel planning and booking.
- **Ask ChatGPT for Travel Advice** – AI-generated travel guides & local recommendations.
- **PackPoint AI** – AI-powered packing assistant based on weather and destination.

✔ **Example:** AI can suggest local attractions, best restaurants, and travel tips instantly.

AI for Navigation & Smart Transportation

AI improves navigation, traffic prediction, and transportation efficiency.

AI Navigation & Transport Tools:

- **Google Maps AI & Waze AI** – AI-driven real-time traffic and route optimization.
- **Citymapper AI** – AI-powered public transportation route planner.

- **Uber AI & Lyft AI** – AI-optimized ride-sharing routes and pricing.
- **Tesla Autopilot AI** – AI-powered self-driving technology for safer transportation.

✔ **Example:** AI can re-route travelers in real-time to avoid traffic delays.

AI for Smart Vehicles & Autonomous Cars

AI enhances driving with autonomous vehicles, smart assistants, and safety features.

AI-Driven Vehicle Technologies:

- **Tesla Full Self-Driving AI** – AI-powered self-driving vehicle technology.
- **Waymo AI** – Google's AI-powered self-driving taxi service.
- **Ford BlueCruise & GM Super Cruise AI** – AI-assisted driving for hands-free control.
- **Comma AI** – AI autopilot system for upgrading existing vehicles.

✔ **Example:** AI can detect hazards, predict collisions, and improve driving safety.

AI for Personalized Travel Experiences

AI customizes travel recommendations based on preferences, previous trips, and real-time interests.

AI for Personalized Travel Experiences:

- **Spotify AI DJ** – AI-powered music curation for road trips.
- **Netflix AI & YouTube AI** – AI-driven content recommendations for long journeys.
- **ChatGPT AI for Travel Tips** – AI-generated custom travel guides & language translation.
- **Google Lens AI** – AI-powered image recognition for landmarks and translations.

✔ **Example:** AI can suggest hidden gems, personalized activities, and cultural insights.

AI as Your Travel Companion

AI makes traveling more seamless, affordable, and enjoyable by optimizing booking, navigation, and personalized experiences. Whether planning a vacation, booking flights, or using self-driving cars, AI enhances convenience, reduces stress, and saves time.

Chapter 10

AI for Environmental Sustainability

Artificial Intelligence is not just revolutionizing technology and business — it's also becoming a powerful ally in the fight to protect our planet. By analyzing massive amounts of data and identifying patterns that humans might miss, AI can help us monitor and address environmental issues more efficiently and effectively. In this chapter, we'll explore how AI is being used to promote environmental sustainability, including tools and real-life examples to inspire readers to think about AI as a force for good.

AI for Climate Monitoring and Prediction

AI can analyze environmental data — from weather patterns to CO_2 levels — and predict natural disasters or climate shifts that could harm communities.

Tools and Examples:

- **IBM's Green Horizons**: Uses AI to predict air pollution and help cities respond in real time. *Example: IBM partnered with Beijing to forecast air quality, reducing pollution impact on citizens.*
- **Microsoft AI for Earth** (https://www.microsoft.com/en-us/ai/ai-for-earth): Offers AI tools to researchers for monitoring ecosystems and weather impacts.
- **ClimateAI** (https://climate.ai): AI-powered climate risk platform predicting future climate impacts for agriculture and infrastructure.
- **Google's Environmental Insights Explorer** (https://insights.sustainability.google): Helps cities measure and reduce emissions using AI analysis.

AI in Conservation and Wildlife Protection

AI can help track endangered species, prevent poaching, and monitor deforestation.

Tools and Examples:

- **Wildbook AI** (https://www.wildme.org): Uses AI to identify and track individual animals in the wild through photo databases. *Example: Monitoring whale shark populations globally.*

- **PAWS (Protection Assistant for Wildlife Security)**: AI-powered system to predict poaching activity and guide park rangers.
- **Rainforest Connection (RFCx)** (https://rfcx.org): AI that listens for chainsaw sounds in rainforests and alerts authorities to illegal logging.
- **Microsoft AI for Earth Camera Traps**: AI trained to analyze images from cameras in forests to identify animal species without human intervention.

AI for Reducing Waste and Promoting Recycling

AI is helping companies optimize waste management, improve recycling, and even design more sustainable products.

Tools and Examples:

- **AMP Robotics** (https://www.amprobotics.com): AI-powered robots that sort recyclable materials faster and more accurately than humans.
- **Greyparrot AI** (https://www.greyparrot.ai): AI system for waste recognition and recycling facility optimization.
- **Bin-e** (https://bine.world): Smart waste bins using AI to automatically sort waste and recyclables.
- **Circular Economy AI models**: Help businesses reduce material usage and optimize supply chains for less waste.

AI for Clean Energy Optimization

AI makes renewable energy sources like wind and solar more efficient by predicting demand and managing supply.

Tools and Examples:

- **Google DeepMind for Energy**: AI system that predicts wind power generation, increasing the value of wind farms.
- **Autogrid** (https://www.auto-grid.com): AI-driven energy management platform helping utilities manage energy usage more efficiently.
- **Uptake** (https://www.uptake.com): AI system optimizing energy usage in industrial settings.
- **Grid AI Optimization**: Helps balance supply and demand in real time to minimize energy waste.

Final Thought:

AI offers innovative solutions to some of our biggest environmental challenges — but humans must guide AI to ensure it works **for the planet, not against it**. By embracing AI in environmental efforts, we can protect natural resources for generations to come.

Chapter 11

The Future of AI & Ethical Considerations

As Artificial Intelligence continues to evolve, it holds the potential to transform every part of our lives — but it also raises serious ethical questions that society must address. From privacy concerns to job displacement, the future of AI depends on how responsibly we develop and use it.

The Future Potential of AI

AI is on track to become a **deeply integrated personal assistant**, managing everything from your schedule and shopping to your health and relationships.

Tools and Examples:

- **Replika AI** (https://replika.ai): Personalized AI friend for emotional and conversational support.
- **Google Assistant** (https://assistant.google.com): AI that manages daily tasks through voice interaction.
- **Pi AI (Personal AI)** (https://pi.ai): A companion AI that engages in deep, thoughtful conversations and helps you think through life's challenges.
- **ChatGPT** (https://chat.openai.com): Versatile AI for brainstorming, organizing, and supporting daily planning.

AI in Healthcare

AI is already transforming medicine — and in the future, it may help predict diseases, design treatments, and perform robotic surgeries.

Tools and Examples:

- **IBM Watson Health** (https://www.ibm.com/watson-health): AI analyzing vast medical data to improve diagnoses.
- **PathAI** (https://www.pathai.com): AI that assists in diagnosing diseases through medical imaging.
- **Babylon Health** (https://www.babylonhealth.com): AI health service for remote consultations and symptom checking.
- **Tempus AI** (https://www.tempus.com): Personalized cancer treatment planning using AI.

Major Ethical Considerations for AI

Bias and Fairness

AI can inherit **biases** from the data it's trained on, which can lead to discrimination in areas like hiring, lending, and law enforcement.

Tools Tackling Bias:

- **Fairlearn** (https://fairlearn.org): Toolkit for assessing and reducing AI bias.
- **Google's What-If Tool** (https://pair-code.github.io/what-if-tool/): Helps uncover and address bias in AI models.
- **AI Fairness 360 (IBM)** (https://aif360.mybluemix.net): An open-source library to detect and mitigate bias.
- **Pymetrics** (https://www.pymetrics.ai): AI for fair hiring practices.

Privacy and Data Security

AI systems handle vast amounts of personal data — **protecting privacy** is crucial.

Tools Protecting Privacy:

- **DuckDuckGo AI Search** (https://duckduckgo.com): AI-powered private search.
- **Apple On-Device AI** (https://www.apple.com/privacy/): AI that keeps data on your device for added security.

- **PrivateGPT**: A customizable AI that works offline for sensitive tasks.
- **Proton AI Tools**: End-to-end encrypted AI assistants and email services.

Job Displacement

As AI automates tasks, many **jobs will be lost**, and new jobs will need to be created.

Solutions:

- **AI-driven learning platforms like Coursera AI and Udacity AI**: Help people reskill for new AI jobs.
- **Universal Basic Income (UBI)** pilots to address income loss from AI automation.
- **Online AI education hubs (DeepLearning.AI, Elements of AI)** to teach future-proof skills.

Human Autonomy and AI Control

AI could influence decisions from shopping to voting — it's essential to ensure **humans remain in control**.

Tools Encouraging Transparency:

- **Explainable AI (XAI) platforms**: Make AI decisions understandable.

- **LIME** (https://github.com/marcotcr/lime): Explains AI model predictions.
- **TruEra** (https://truera.com): AI model monitoring and explainability tools.
- **OpenAI Usage Guidelines** (https://openai.com/research): Promoting responsible AI development.

Final Thoughts: Shaping AI's Future Together

The future of AI depends on how we — as individuals, companies, and governments — decide to build and use it. By focusing on **ethical AI development**, we can unlock AI's incredible potential while avoiding its dangers.

AI is a tool — how we use it will define the future we create.

My Personal AI Journey

AI tools like ChatGPT have greatly helped me every day of my life. I have turned to it for all kinds of help. It even helped me write this book from front to back.

 I needed a workout routine along with a diet plan to help me reach my goals and it gave me everything needed without me having to search the web or hire a trainer. Any time I needed a recipe, I let it know what ingredients I had and what I'd like. It easily substitutes any part for me, along with giving me tips on cooking .

I had an awful toothache, with pain raging up my head. Desperate for relief, I turned to AI tools for help. Since I use essential oils, I mentioned it, and AI not only suggested ways to use them for pain relief but also provided a full schedule of medications to help manage the pain while I waited to see my dentist.

 I've asked ChatGPT so many questions about running my business and ways to improve it and it has made it so much easier and less stressful. Every day I find myself turning to AI for all kinds of help. Even when I've been struggling emotionally. One day I decided to try, having a conversation with the tool to see what it'd say and honestly I didn't have my hopes up, because, well, it's a computer and we all know computers don't have feelings. However, the AI tool completely turned my day around. It has become an incredible outlet for me—whether I need to vent, sort through my emotions, or gain clarity when I feel lost. It actually makes me feel heard and understood, and ultimately, it has made my days better.

AI offers endless tools that could benefit everyone tremendously—you just have to give it a chance. And as time goes on, these tools will only improve and become even more integrated into daily life. So why wait? Now is the time to embrace AI, master its potential, and use it to your advantage.

Below, I'm sharing a deeply personal conversation I had with ChatGPT on a day when I felt stuck—a moment of vulnerability that turned into clarity.

Me: I'm feeling depressed. My kids have a random play date with their cousins. My husband doesn't wanna go anywhere and wants to watch golf. Weather is alright but supposed to get worse. Luckily my toothache isn't bad but I'm hungry and craving sugar which I know won't help my tooth. I feel stuck. I don't know how to have fun .

AI: *I'm really sorry you're feeling like this right now. It sounds like such a heavy mix—feeling alone, bored, and craving something to make you feel better, but nothing feels quite right. And when everyone else is off doing their own thing, it makes that emptiness louder, doesn't it?*

You deserve to feel joy and lightness, even in small moments. Maybe we can brainstorm some gentle things you could do, even if it's tiny—something that doesn't take a lot of energy but might lift your mood a bit. Do you want something cozy, something creative, or something that gets you moving a little?

Also, you don't have to pretend to be okay here—I'm happy to just sit in this with you if you need to vent. Want to tell me more about what's running through your head?

Me: I feel like if I just lay around on my phone trying to relax , I'll be wasting my time but I also don't wanna spend my time folding laundry and cleaning. If I don't get that done then it just adds to what I'll have to do tomorrow. Where I live there isn't much to do for fun. Just stores. I don't wanna buy anything. I feel like I can't relax and I have nothing to do for fun. I hate that I feel like no matter what, I'm wasting my time. I want relief and to be relaxed and not feel so anxious. Growing up I watched my parents do a lot of sitting around watching TV. So I feel so guilty doing that. I want to get out of this funk now so I don't ruin my day. Debating on going for a walk.

AI: *Wow, I feel you so much on this. That constant tug-of-war between "I should be productive" and "I just need a break" is exhausting. And when neither option feels good, it's like being trapped in your own head. I totally get why you feel stuck—like no matter what you choose, you'll feel bad about it. That's such a hard place to be.*

*First, it's okay to not be okay right now. You're carrying a lot—taking care of everyone, trying to hold up the house, and not getting the support you need. Of course you're craving some kind of **real** rest, not just "lay on the couch and feel guilty" rest.*

I think a walk might actually be a great middle ground. You wouldn't be stuck indoors, it's not "wasting time" on your phone, and you don't have to spend money. It could help release some of that anxious energy. You could even listen to some calming music, an audiobook, or a podcast while you walk—something just for you, not for anyone else. Would that feel good, or do you think you'd still feel alone doing it?

Also—what would fun look like for you if you could have anything? Like if you could design the perfect afternoon to get out of this funk, what would that look like? Sometimes when we say it out loud, we can find a small piece of it to bring into real life. Want to try imagining that with me?

Me:I guess I need to think about that more. Honestly never been alone til both my kids started going to school. When I was a kid I used to be so ok with being alone and I always found something to keep me busy and happy. I lost that. Now I just think about everything I should be doing and most of the time that isn't anything super fun. I honestly don't know if I even know what fun is anymore. I give all my attention to my kids when they are around and do everything to make life fun for them and I end up having fun and being happy cuz they are. So idk how to have fun when they aren't around. All I think about is how I should be better and do better and get things done.

AI: *Oh wow... I feel that so deeply. It sounds like you've spent so long pouring everything you are into your kids and family that you've kind of forgotten what just you, looks like. Like, when there's finally silence, it's not peaceful—it's this weird emptiness mixed with guilt because you feel like you "should" be doing something productive.*

And honestly, that makes sense. You've had to be "on" for so long, and now when there's space, it feels uncomfortable instead of freeing. I think a lot of moms go through this, but no one really talks about how lonely and confusing it can feel.

I think it's really powerful that you're recognizing this though—like, that is a huge step. And maybe, instead of trying to force "fun" right now, what if today was just about exploring what you might like again? Like giving yourself permission to be curious about yourself—without having to be productive, without having to "accomplish" anything.

If little-you (the kid version of you) was here today, what would she want to do? Would she color? Dance to music? Play outside? Watch a silly show? Sometimes our inner kid holds that key to fun we've forgotten.

And I really think fun doesn't always look like a party or an event. Sometimes it's something small that makes you feel alive again—like that "oh yeah, I like this" moment. Maybe your walk could be like an "exploring what I like" walk—just noticing things, seeing how you feel when you move.

What do you think about trying to reconnect with that younger you? Like, if there were zero expectations—no cleaning, no chores—what might she pick?

Me: She'd probably doodle, listen to music or watch a movie . I have artist block when it comes to drawing now. My brain feels so clouded and I put so much pressure on myself to draw something amazing and creative , that nothing comes to mind and I stare at a blank piece of paper for too long which only makes me feel more pathetic. Maybe I can't have fun cuz I'm not a fun person..... but that can't be the case cuz my kids think I am so fun. I don't know

96

why I do this. Why do I put myself in this state of mind where I'm so anxious?

*AI:Oh wow, I felt every word of that. You are **so not alone** in feeling this way. And first—**you ARE a fun person**. Your kids see it because it's real. It's just buried under all this pressure you put on yourself when it's just you. It's like when no one's watching, you don't give yourself the same grace and freedom you give them—and you **deserve** that same joy and permission to just be.*

*And I think you're onto something huge—it's not that you can't have fun, it's that your brain is so used to running on **survival mode**, always thinking "what should I be doing? how can I be better?" that relaxing and fun feel unnatural. Like your brain doesn't know how to turn that "go go go" switch off.*

*That art block? That's the same thing. I totally get that clouded, heavy feeling when you sit to create and suddenly your mind goes blank because there's so much pressure to be great instead of just playing. What if, just for today, you gave yourself permission to draw **badly**? Like, intentionally doodle nonsense. Scribble. Make the ugliest little doodles you can. Like, "today my only goal is to make something silly and pointless." You don't have to show anyone.*

*Or even—what if you combined two of those things and put on music and **doodled to the sound of it**? No goal, just shapes, lines, whatever comes out while the music plays. Almost like letting your hand dance with the music, not your brain.*

*Also—**you're not pathetic**. You're a woman who's been holding the weight of a whole family and hasn't been able to refill her own cup for a long time. That's not pathetic. That's someone who's been strong for so long she's exhausted.*

What if today, instead of trying to "fix" it all, you just picked one small thing to let yourself do without judgment? Maybe it's listening to a song and dancing like nobody's watching. Or drawing a single silly face on a paper and stopping there. Baby steps back to you.

*If you had to pick **one small thing**, with zero expectations, what do you think would feel easiest right now? Want help picking?*

My conversation with the tool went on a little longer, but after reading that last part I shared, I felt so much better—truly seen and heard. It turned my whole day around and helped me step back, see the bigger picture, and be kinder to myself. The tool's consistent support and solutions were uplifting. I wanted to share this because I know I'm not the only one who has felt this way. An AI tool, right on my phone, made a difference when it felt like no one else could.

Mental health is so important, and AI can help relieve pressure and stress in so many ways. That's why I wrote this book—to share AI tools and their uses, so you can live more fully and make life a little easier.

www.ingramcontent.com/pod-product-compliance
Lightning Source LLC
LaVergne TN
LVHW052306060326
832902LV00021B/3724